Conversations of a Mother

Conversations of a Mother

Brianna L. Denning-Spencer

© 2022 Brianna L. Denning-Spencer

ISBN-978-0-578-34687-8
ALL RIGHTS RESERVED
Library of Congress Control Number: 2022904011
Mountain Top Publishing LLC, Paducah, KY

No Portion of this manuscript may be reproduced in any fashion, photocopy, film, or published form without written permission from it's publisher or the author.

Produced by MOUNTAINTOP PUBLISHING, LLC
P.O. Box 7287 Paducah, KY. 42002-7287
mountaintoppublish@bellsouth.net

In Memoriam:

Granny

(Rosetta Smith Edmondson),

Aunt Jeri

(Margaret Geraldine McCatty),

Granddaddy

(James Edward Sawyers),

Dear

(Annie Pearl Sawyers).

Rest with Jesus,

My Angels

Special Dedication:

Ms. Victoria Johnson,

Thank you for being who you are!
I love you, Cousin!

Special Thanks:

To all the readers: thank you for starting the conversation. It's not easy to discuss, understand, or win; however, once it starts, it won't stop. Try listening beyond what is said, listen through the emotions; listen for the heart.
At the end of Luke 6:45 it reads "out of the heart, the mouth speaks".

To my Momm-E Friends whom I talked to, who talked back, cried, and listened. The ones who completed the surveys or interviews; our conversations, the ones who referred me to others that they knew went through this. Thank you for your words of encouragement, your criticisms, sharing your truths, and most of all your heart!

To Ms. Sara Evans, Dr. Stephen McLeod-Bryant, Lady Shanae Edwards, Mrs. Kierra Bogus, The Freeman's, Mr. Jonathan Snorten, Bishop Kelvin

Leavy Sr., Lady Chonta Leavy, and District Elder Anthony Walton; I am grateful for all of you!

To my family: this process was a struggle but thank you for putting up with me. I'm sure the many mood swings weren't easy; however, I am truly grateful for you loving me in spite of me.

Spencer 3, thank you for being everything you are to me. Thank you for challenging, pushing, encouraging, and loving me throughout EVERYTHING!
Thank you for ALWAYS being my beautiful surprise!

Foreword

Back in the day when we used to think of motherhood, we would look at those mothers on television, the Huxtables, the Cleavers, the Winslow's, the Brady's, the Browns, etc. Then we began to face the reality that we have examples of motherhood all around us that should be given recognition, prayers, and praise.

Motherhood is not a "one size fits most." Each mother is on a journey of her own but doesn't have to walk it alone. We read about Biblical mothers Hannah, Mary, Naomi, Eunice, and Lois and find they had specific walks and their struggles knowing they didn't understand what the end would be "but God." However, they did not shirk their responsibilities. They had conversations with the Lord for direction. I don't believe the conversations were always easy but were received.

The vision given to Brianna L. Spencer for a compilation of the life experiences of these special women is great. As the author said "Yes," to God, she trusted Him to provide the vessels for this writing. As God gives the wisdom to seek those with a testimony, we are moved to learn how not to be judgmental but to empathize with the different circumstances and something to want to embrace them. These mothers are those who may be in a struggle or have struggled but they never gave up.

As a mother, I've wrestled with some of the things some of them were going through and will go through. I appreciate them for being available and being transparent. "Each mother was in "that season" of her life." This book, *Conversations of a Mother*, will open to the reader the complexity of motherhood as well as the joy it can bring. Brianna was blessed to have conversations with these mothers. Some who did not have her experiences, some with similar experiences and some were unique.

Our family was blessed to have five living generations of mothers, motherly aunts and cousins, nieces, and Godmothers, etc. We were taught to keep God first and to be the example for our daughters, etc. The author, Brianna takes her role as a wife, mother, aunt, cousin, friend, and a child of God as a gift. The love we received from our own mothers had a power of its own.

A true mother's love is unconditional, limitless and includes discipline, protection and prayer helps you through those tough times.

Brianna is a mother who knows how it is to "mother" others. She has seen many examples and is learning by experience. There is no way to be a perfect mother, just continually ask for Godly wisdom and guidance and not wallow in what you can't control. Her very nature afforded each participant the freedom to freely express themselves and share their story.

Yes, sometimes circumstances hurt, and tears are shed. That thing called "fear" occasionally injects itself and tries to derail our plans. Now and then a mother admitting she's wrong or has to be strong in horrific circumstances can test her. Helping clean up after a sick child or helping with homework or accepting who she is as a mother and facing things life handed her makes us part of the "village" a mother needs just as it takes a village to raise a child. Then comes the time when your children bring you those flowers (weeds) and present them with so much love, makes everything worthwhile.

Brianna has been in several of these situations. She made the choice of motherhood and places her children's needs above her own. It isn't always easy, but she believes she "can do all things through Christ that strengthens her." With that thought, she exhibits the virtues of learning the daily lessons of motherhood and puts them into practice.

Her prayer is that even in their various situations these beautiful women will remember they are "blessed among women."

As you read this book, I pray that you will be encouraged by their testimonies and appreciate knowing that regardless of their experiences – the love they exude is still that of a mother.

Dr. Glenda L. Dunlap, Th.D.

Preface

Conversation: an exchange of thoughts, information, etc., by spoken or written words, between people.

This book was birthed out of conversations with different sister friends and family members who recently gave birth or were pregnant. They expressed their thoughts about love, pregnancy, post-pregnancy, becoming a mother, back-to-back children, and getting back to loving themselves. During all the changes that come along with pregnancy and becoming a mother, this can be difficult to do.

Each experience is different, so this may or may not help you. Because you too, will overcome this! His word declares that YOU will overcome by the blood of the Lamb and the word of your testimony.
This is just a series of conversations between friends, mothers.

I hope this will help you start a conversation with your families and other mothers.

Welcome to my thoughts, feelings, issues, and prayers that helped me WIN. Prayers of self-acceptance, peace, new mothers, freedom, and Thanksgiving. If you have faith and fight in you, you can and WILL WIN!

Let's start talking….

Opening Prayer for the Reader:

*Lord, I thank You for making me! I thank You for each new day that You have allowed me to see. Thank You for creating obstacles for me to overcome! Revelations 12:11 it reads, **we** overcome by the blood of the Lamb and the word of our testimony!*

I have overcome it naturally and spiritually through Your grace! Your favor has propelled me into this destiny that I walk in daily! Thank You for walking me through my tests and trials. Although I thought I couldn't, I did all things through You! And for that I am forever Yours! Let my thoughts be your thoughts, and my ways be Your ways!

Lord, I thank You for the woman, man, mother, father, son, and daughter who is reading this book. Open their minds to begin to think positive. Open their ears to hear you clearly. Help them to hear through the words written on this page. Open their hearts to love as You love us. Show them how to love their families with the love of Christ.

Open their mouths to speak life, no longer speaking harmful things to damage people. Father, help us to no longer destroy ourselves or others with our words and actions.

I pray that through this book their knowledge is increased. I pray that they begin to show kindness to their loved ones, that wasn't shown before due to misunderstandings. I pray that in the moment of weakness, they show strength and love for their loved ones. Show them how to love unconditionally like You.

I decree and declare in Jesus name that the devil will no longer have a place in their hearts and minds! That the strongholds that they face daily will no longer reside in their hearts and minds.

In Jesus' Name we pray!
Amen.

Chapters:

Chapter 1:
I'm What?? That's what the Doctor said...

Conversation with a Mother with an unborn baby

Conversation with a New Mother

Conversation with a Girl Mom

Prayer for New Mothers

Chapter 2:
My weight does not define ME!

Conversation with a Single Mother who Dealt with Trauma

Conversation with a Single Mother

Prayer of Self-Acceptance

Chapter 3:
It just got REAL!!!!

Conversation with a Mother of Young Children

Conversation with a Mother that has Battled Depression

Conversation with a Mother of a High School Boy

Table of Contents continued...

Prayer of Peace

<u>Chapter 4:</u>
Walking in Victory
Prayer of Freedom
Prayer of Thanksgiving
Encouraging Words
Closing prayer

Chapter 1:

"I'm What??" That's what the Doctor said . . .

Every girl dream of being married, having children, and a career! Well, at least the ones I know. Now for me, I'm not too sure I recall wanting all of that; traveling was a priority for me. I know I wanted to be successful in whatever I pursued, but I don't really recall wanting marriage or a baby. Little did I know God's plan for my life would be different.

My husband and I had only been married roughly four years when we decided to move back to Tennessee from Colorado. The decision was easy because we missed our family and friends. We had to make some adjustments when we returned, which in hindsight was very good. When we came back, we were so excited to be among those who could help us in our marriage.

Over the course of our marriage, we discussed having children, but with no definite timeline. We were more in the mindset of "if it happens it happens", but we really didn't consider ourselves ready. Who is? Let's be honest. You can be financially prepared to care for a child, but not necessarily emotionally or spiritually ready. I also knew that I wasn't ready to give up my physical body. For my body to be invaded, yes invaded, by another person.

Again, God's plan is much different.

Almost ten years ago, I had a feeling that my life was changing. There were several days where I felt uneasy, uncomfortable, and queasy. I thought, "I know my body, why am I feeling this way?"

So, I had a conversation with my mother. She suggested that I ask for a pregnancy test during my upcoming annual visit. My response to her was:

I said: "Mama, for real?"

Mom said: "Well, we will probably have two at the same time".

Me: "Wait, what? I said."

Mom replies: (as she ignored my question) "Just do it. You never know."

So, I did. Unbeknownst to me, someone in my family was pregnant at the same time and everyone was not aware yet. My test came back as a false positive. Which means the test was inconclusive, so the nurse suggested that I get a blood test to check my levels. That day, I left the office and decided to continue my daily routine.

Now, we play the waiting game until Monday. She called two days later and said that my levels have increased and asked if I could come back for a follow-up test. Another test? I mean really, you're gonna prick me again? I responded, "I guess." I now wait two more days for the results of Blood Test #2. She called and said my levels increased, but the doctor said it might be too early to tell. Now back to the doctor for one more blood test. I guess the third time was a charm. I really did not know how to feel. At this point, I am still not doing well physically. I still have days of queasiness, days of anxiousness, and I began to crave random things.

When I went back to the doctor, I received the biggest shock of my life. "Mrs. Spencer," she said, "your hormones have tripled and yes, you are pregnant." Oh, um, ok, Great! Pregnant? What does that look like? My first thought, *I'm about to be fat! Really!!!*

As the months progressed, during one of the doctor's visits, I was told that I would have to get a cesarean section. *Excuse me! Why?* A C-section! I began to feel so many emotions right there in the doctor's office. I was fearful and overwhelmed. I felt as if I had done something wrong in my body. I felt as if I was not having a baby the "proper" way. Proper in the sense of a vaginal birth. All I had ever heard was women having a baby vaginally, and I thought I was not woman enough. Key word is thought! Which was absolutely wrong! No one in my family had ever had a C-section. I honestly did not know what to expect. The doctor mentioned that my pelvic bones were too small to birth a 7-pound baby. So, for my health this was the best and safest option.

I recall a conversation with one of the young moms at church who had two C-sections. She told me her experience. She told me that it was hard, and how peaceful it was. All she remembered was the calmness during all the chaos in the operating room.

I had to gather myself in preparation for the birth. Although still apprehensive, I knew all would be well.

Between working long hours and being overly exhausted all the time, food was my best friend.

I desired sweets, Nestle Crunch bars and Key lime pie with almond brickle. The cravings that I desired most were bologna & cheese sandwiches with a bowl of cereal. No, they did not physically go together but it just seemed right.

When you're pregnant, who's to say what's wrong or what things shouldn't go together. However, the foods that I once loved at that time had the most horrid smell, such as grilled tilapia or steamed crab. All those things I loved so much, after the first trimester, I could eat, and the smell would not bother me.

When I was a little over four months pregnant, I had to go to the emergency room because I was severely dehydrated. Due to working so much, I failed to take care of myself in the process. After that brief hospital visit, I made a point to slow down, and make sure I ate well and drank plenty of fluids.

When I made it to the second trimester my food cravings increased, my body began changing. My feet ached all the time and my back began throbbing. I even experienced sciatic nerve spasms that would start at my lower back, then to my butt and go down my leg; but I made it.

At a little over eight months, I went into labor. In all actuality I had been in labor that entire day. I was in pain and tired. I drove to meet the pediatrician. The pediatrician told me at the time that I needed to go home and rest.

Being obedient, I went home to rest for a few hours, but then I went to pick up my niece, and I started to have contractions while driving home. She knew something was not right and began to freak out. She called my mom, and she came over to make sure I was ok. Later that evening all I could think about was the nice vegetable lasagna that mom cooked that Wednesday before church.

I was preparing to go to church with my sister and my niece, and my mom struck up a conversation with my sister Chae and me.

"Brianna, what are you doing?" Mama asked.
"Getting ready for church," I said.
"Why? Insert that mom, raised eyebrow look". You are in labor." she said
"No, I'm not, I'm just in a little pain. I will be fine!" I said as a contraction brings me to my knees.
"Who is taking you?" Mama asked.
"I'm not driving; Chae came to pick me up. I'll be fine," I said.
"You really don't need to go! Chae, please call her doctor if she is contracting every 5-10 minutes!" she said, slightly irritated.
"Okay," Chae said.

My sister and I made it to church where most of the time was spent outside on the steps, or in the bathroom while having more contractions. At that time, I had two amazing women that got me through the contractions.

C: You know you're having this baby, right?
Me: No, I'm not. (truly in denial, while having another contraction). But I'm hungry.
S: No, you need to quit thinking about food. Your baby is coming tonight.
Me: Laughing while having more contractions.
They laughed with and at me until I decided to go to the hospital. They, like my mom, said I should have stayed home; but I really wanted to go to church.

I arrived at the hospital, and after getting checked in, my husband and I found out that I was 6 centimeters dilated. Labor was extremely painful! I mean extremely painful. I was just supposed to get a c-section and not feel any of this. But no, God decided that my handsome little guy was coming that night. He made his debut a week early at 10:20pm. He weighed 7 pounds and 3 ounces, and18 inches long. His name, *God's gift*, truly showed me how precious life is and how awesome God is for giving him to us.

During that time, my husband and I were taught lessons in patience, grace, and love so much more than our hearts could contain. Our son became a caring, gentle, kind boy that we learned from every day. We thought we were fine with one child, but God had another plan for us.

In December 2012, I started to feel sick. Most sicknesses were sinus infections, migraine headaches, and body aches daily. I really did not know what was going on. I was literally sick for several months. At that time, I think back and don't remember a menstrual cycle occurring. I remember sitting on the side of the bed while my husband was in the bathroom. "Babe, I don't remember having my cycle," I said. "Well, go to the doctor and see if you're pregnant," he replied.

I went to the doctor, and again heard "Mrs. Spencer, you are indeed pregnant!" *I'm what?? Oh Lord, what am I going to do now?!* All the emotions came flooding back; I was so overwhelmed. That afternoon I ate a half dozen donuts. I called my mom and my sister and told them. *They* were very excited. *I* cried for three days and ate everything I could get my hands on.

I cried and cried Not because I didn't want another child, but because I was just not ready to have another one so soon. My oldest son was not even one. He was still in diapers, not even walking yet, and here I am pregnant, AGAIN! At the time of delivery, they would be sixteen months apart. Those emotions would clearly carry over into the pregnancy, and life would take its toll on me.

The weight of this pregnancy was much different. Life began to get increasingly busier. After a visit to the doctor, I realized that I was 11 weeks pregnant. Every month of my pregnancy it seemed as if something different was going wrong. At that time, I lost an aunt, who was out of state, which was extremely hard. I could not travel to be with my family when they laid her to rest. After that my husband's car was involved in a hit and run at our apartment complex. They stated that they could do nothing about it. I was frustrated and overwhelmed. Then, the baby's heartbeat became irregular, and every appointment that I went to my blood pressure was elevated. I was very concerned and mentally exhausted.

As if that was not enough, I slipped and fell at work. Physical therapy was not much of an option because I was too far along in the pregnancy. I was told to do stretches. At that point I just wanted to cry. I was in pain and there was not much that could be done. Mentally I was drained. Finally, my best friend's doctor found a spot on her lung, another huge blow. I got that news, and, like most people, I began to fear the worst. All I could do was cry and ask God why so much was going on.

Although it was a lot going on in my life, I knew I had to continue. but we made it!
We have been through so much, and our little one wasn't even here yet. This warrior was my strength and helped me fight daily.

Through it all, we fought together! We found out we were having another boy. We chose a name for him that clearly defined who God was in our lives. God was and is our Savior. Only He could have kept me and my son through all of this. His name means, *"The Lord is my God and salvation."*

During the delivery I began to get sick. I vomited while on the table during the c-section, but my warrior fought through. He came out at 11:06 am, 7 pounds and 6 ounces, and 19 inches long. God blessed us with another healthy and handsome baby boy.

After his arrival things began to change. My emotions were everywhere. Hormones were raging.

I was happy and then sad. Then there were days of feeling afraid and hopeless. At times I was extremely angry. I didn't know what to do with myself. I tried my best to mask my feelings the best way I could.

My pain and hormones were so intense. I knew things would be different. My life has changed, not just physically but mentally, emotionally, and most of all spiritually.

I read this quote by Rachel Martin.
"Motherhood is messy. And challenging. And crazy. And sleepless. And giving. And still unbelievably beautiful."

This quote spoke volumes to me. There are daily situations that mothers tend to that are messy. Such as blow-out diapers, baby food splatters, spit up on everything except the bib, and the list goes on. Then there are the challenges of keeping life organized. The crazy times where you are running around trying to keep up with your child and you just can't. Or the sleepless nights when your little one is teething or has gas and can't sleep. Or when you give and give, and it seems as if you are so depleted that you have nothing else to give. Then there is the most beautiful moment; the time you take to reflect.

When you look at your baby and they look at you and your heart just melt. Seeing something so precious that you created, in your arms just reminds you how beautiful life is.

Conversation of a Mother with an Unborn baby

B: How has your pregnancy been?

C: A ROLLERCOASTER!! I say that because it's my first pregnancy and I didn't know what to expect. Some things I went through that my friends didn't go through. The last leg of my pregnancy has been very emotional and painful.

B: Why emotional?

C: My emotions are all over the place, and I just don't understand why.

B: What are your fears about becoming a mother?

C: Not knowing what I am doing, but I know that my instincts will kick in when it's time. Also having to care for another human being.

B: You're gonna be a great mom! What are you most excited about?

C: Seeing her grow up. Watching her personality. What she will become as she is raised by my husband and me. I look forward to spending time with her and learning all there is to know about her.

Conversation with a New Mother

B: Was there anything challenging about your pregnancy?

S: Absolutely! I developed gestational diabetes. I had to stick myself with needles 4-6 times a day. At the end I developed preeclampsia and high blood pressure, and that took me to preterm labor.

B: Did the high blood pressure and diabetes continue after she was born?

S: As soon as I delivered all those things were gone.

B: As a mother, do you feel like you had everything together as far as after the birth?

S: Absolutely not! I felt like I was prepared, until she came at 36 weeks and the doctor said, "you're having the baby today!" I asked the doctor if I could go home and get my stuff, she said no, and things got real really quickly. That day my blood pressure was super high!

B: Did you ever experience postpartum depression?

S: Yes, ma'am I did.

B: What did that look like to you?

S: I was sad and cried a lot. My husband held me, and I cried so hard as if I lost my best friend or something.

B: How did you get through the postpartum depression?

S: I got over it around the 4–5-week mark, but I still have moments where I feel overwhelmed.

B: Feeling overwhelmed is normal. What would you say to new mothers?

S: Follow your heart! Sometimes you don't feel like you know what you are doing, but you are doing a good job! You'll figure it all out! It takes time!

Conversation with a Girl Mom

B: Have you ever experienced postpartum depression? What did that look/ feel like to you?
R: I have. To me it looked like I was very drained. I had low energy. Almost like I was in a cloud of despair lingering above my head.
B: When you mention a cloud, can you elaborate on that?
R: I felt like it was very spiritual. I was breastfeeding and already tired. And when you are naturally drained it can open the door to a very dark place spiritually. What I mean by that is when you are breastfeeding and already tired, you can find yourself thinking negative thoughts. And I would allow myself to think that I was a bad mother or that I was not good enough. One specific thought was "this is all that I am good for, this is all I'm useful for". I had to catch it myself, because I knew I was better than what I may have felt or tried to make myself believe.
B: How did you get through it?

R: Prayer. I had to realize it at that moment. I would go into a blank stare, but it helped to communicate with my husband how I was feeling after the last pregnancy. I also had to make an effort to do things to make me happy. I experienced depression 3 out of 4 pregnancies.

B: How is it being a girl mom?

R: It's great! I feel like I have people I can shape from my own experiences. I know what they deal with. I can make them great women.

B: You're doing a great job.

R: By the grace of God.

B: Did you experience any trauma or issues during any of your pregnancies? How did you handle it?

R: Yes, with my blood pressure. It would increase after I would get home from having the babies, which would lead to me getting hospitalized. Doctors did not know why, but I was determined not to go back to the hospital. Fortunately, I was able to have medication so that I did not have to go into the hospital.

Prayer for New Mothers

Lord, I thank You for making my womb fruitful! Thank You for trusting me to raise <u>speak Your child(ren)'s name</u> in the fear and admonition of you. Give me the strength to cover my child(ren) in prayer and to intercede in the spirit on their behalf. 1 Peter 5:7 says "Father, give me the insight to cast all my cares on You because you care for me. "Help me to understand how to use the weapons of the spirit to fight and win the wars of my everyday life.

Through the power of Jesus Christ, I pull down every stronghold of postpartum depression. I bind up every manifestation of the spirit of fear, in Jesus' name. Father, I decree that I operate in patience, love, and peace when disciplining my children. I decree that I will have supernatural energy and stamina to take care of my family and to provide for my household. I decree that the daily routine of caring for my household will bring me joy and pleasure.

Now, Lord, I dedicate my life to You. My children belong to You. My home belongs to You. My heart belongs to You. The weapons of my warfare are ready to be used! You are my strength and my song as I enter motherhood.

In Jesus' Name,
Amen.

Chapter 2:

My weight doesn't define me

I never struggled so much with my weight, until after my children were born. I was always curvy, always thick. To be honest, I was fine with the way I looked. After the birth of my first son, I bounced back to my pre-baby weight right after delivery. That was the most amazing thing to me. I breastfed, losing quite a bit of weight. I worked crazy hours and still had time to be super mom. Weight and good health were not as much of a concern to me, but after the birth of my second son things didn't go back to how they were.

It was as if my body shifted, and I couldn't fit things like I did before. The weight took its time coming off, and it's still taking some time to come off. Things didn't fit like they used to, and in turn my image of myself wasn't the same. We are our own worst critics and as a new mom, I tore myself up. I belittled myself. I degraded myself. I felt as if I were much larger than I appeared. My mind tried to play so many tricks on me. Your mind can be a blessing and a curse when dealing with your issues. Prior to the pregnancies, there were never issues with my self-confidence; however, my confidence was surely shaken after the birth of my children.

I can't blame them for my weight, that was solely my issue. When you begin to think about your weight, you instantly compare yourself to other women. You must take a step back and realize their bodies are not yours, and vice versa. I honestly compared myself too.

Seriously, I would compare myself to most women. Some didn't have children, and some did. I remember sitting down and watching TV. There was a woman who had just had a baby 9 weeks prior, and she was super skinny. It's almost as if she could have been on a weight loss commercial. I thought to myself, *why can't I be like her? Why is she so special to God, that she can just bounce back? What's wrong with me? What am I not doing that she is?*

That image disturbed me! Yet, I continued to eat and eat. I over indulged while comparing myself to someone that cared nothing about me; someone who probably did not have two children back-to-back. Someone who probably had a personal trainer ready after her 6-week check-up. Self-comparison can be a dangerous thing. It can lead to desires and realities that you are not ready to face.

One of my insecurities was that I felt like I was not good enough anymore. I thought, *would my husband love me like I am now?* But what was realistic is my opinion of myself. So many days I had to fight all the negative thoughts. The thoughts some days would overwhelm me. But I had to start speaking positively and encouraging myself. Then I had to realize my struggle and perception was solely based on how I felt about myself.

There is a scripture that I began to meditate on, 3 John 1:2 KJV, *"Beloved, I wish above all things that you mayest prosper and be in health, even as thy soul prospereth."* After meditating on that scripture, I remembered that I am the one in control of being healthy and happy. If I want to be healthy and not compare myself to others, then I must start with myself.

I had to re-evaluate several areas of my life. Which included my mind, self-confidence, sleeping pattern, and adding exercise to my daily routine. My self-confidence had to be rebuilt. I had to come to grips with this overindulging in food, which was my personal issue! I came to the realization that I had to correct the problem in me, so that I could be a better version of myself.

The comparison and overeating had to stop.
I had to stop looking at myself as if I were a victim, when in all actuality these things could have been prevented!

I had to retrain my mind that I was enough!
It all was dependent on me and what I was thinking; it had to stop!

It had to stop because it was consuming my every thought. It had to stop because I could not be overweight and happy. I cannot speak for anyone else; I can only speak for me and my experience. I could not function knowing that the things that I put into my body were doing damage. The scripture was so heavy on my heart. God wants us to be in good health and to prosper and I couldn't prosper if I was unhealthy.

I began to receive that in my spirit. I stopped allowing low self-esteem to attack and tear me down. I no longer allowed the enemy to play mind games with me! I became more aware that weight issues and unhealthy choices could be passed down to my children. I was no longer going to allow these to damage my confidence. I stopped playing games within myself!

I chose to be and do better! From this point forward, I started accepting who God created me to be and wanted me to be! I started accepting my body, and all the rolls. I started working toward looking and feeling better.

Next, I had to evaluate my sleeping patterns. As a new mother I realized that I was clearly not getting enough sleep. I really had to make time to rest and stop while my child was sleeping! I started evaluating my eating habits and how much water I was drinking. I also had to be intentional about working out. All four of those things were not a priority to me before because my babies were now my first priority.

I was reminded that if I am not healthy for me, then I may not even be here to take care of my children. If I was not there for my children, then I would not be there for my husband or any member of my family.

So, I knew right then that there were some changes I needed to make. One of which was my diet. I had to incorporate more vegetables, salads, and less red meat. To be honest, during this time I had an unhealthy obsession with food. It made it easy for me to drown myself in all kinds of food. I would fill up with so many emotions that I allowed myself to eat anything. If I was happy, then I'd eat ice cream. If I was upset, then I would eat tacos. If I was sad, then I would make a strawberry cake and eat half of it by myself.

During those times I would allow myself to compare my post-pregnancy self to who I was before, or who I felt I should have been. I had to take several steps back and truly analyze myself.

Once I started examining myself, I had to focus on turning the plate over when I would become emotional. about life's happenings. Things happen, life happens, but it was my response to the emotions that mattered most. I had to be intentionally active. More walking, and in some cases I had to work out. I had to refocus and bring several things back to the forefront to better myself.

Exercise is a great deal of work and necessary. You can exercise your mind, your spirit, and your body. All of which will make for a healthy you. It does take a lot of work, but if you want something bad enough then you must work for it. I recall a brother at the church saying, "You make time for what you want to make time for!" That resonated with me! Although as a new mom balance is a word that is not in your vocabulary, I had to make time to take care of myself.

I began walking with the baby, reading the Bible more, or going to visit with friends. I had to exercise all parts of myself. When we were in a better financial position, I was able to get a manicure or facial just to make me feel good.

My sleep pattern was a struggle altogether. My husband and I worked together to get the baby on a sleep schedule so that I could rest. I know you are asking about *housekeeping, laundry, etc.,* I had the same questions, but I also had to have balance; so, do you. If the baby generally sleeps for two hours, then you sleep for an hour and then you tackle the household duties.

You must start somewhere, or you will be so exhausted; no good to anyone.

I may not be there yet, But I'm closer than I was yesterday.
-Author unknown

Where this is no struggle, there is no strength.
-Oprah Winfrey

Conversations with a Single Mother who dealt with Trauma

B: How do you handle being a single mother?

J: That's a loaded question. I take it day by day. There is no blueprint. I've always seen my mom, grandmother, both single mothers, so I took what I learned from them.

B: What did you take away from your mom and grandmother?

J: Children are not the same as when we were children. The father of one of my children passed away. No one knew how to handle it, but my grandmother did, so I learned so much from her.

B: Your son's father passed? I'm sure that was extremely hard.

J: Yeah, I found out on the news. I was in complete disbelief. I just cried and cried; I was so upset. My son was diagnosed with PTSD. He did not know his dad well, but my son knew something was wrong. He did question his dad's actions that day.

B: How do you maintain your own sanity?

J: I have to watch getting involved with some people, because it just gets too messy. So being by myself sometimes is better than being social and getting involved in a mess.

Conversation with a Single Mother:

B: How is it being a single mother?
D: At times stressful! Times where I want to be by myself, then I start to miss my kids. I enjoy being a single mother. For me, my kids are receiving a better life now, than when I was married. I can rear my children the way I desire and without a lot of negativity.
B: How do you manage taking care of your children and making time for yourself?
D: It's hard to have time for myself. The saying that "it takes a village to raise a child", is so true for me. My family is so supportive of us. My parents, grandparents, aunts all help me when I need a break. Sometimes my family isn't available, and I have to tell my boys, look I need a few minutes to

myself. Please help each other with homework, while I rest.

I do have a health condition, so they respect me when I say I need peace and quiet or time to rest.

B: Tell me a little more about your story.

D: I had my first baby from a rape. I was a virgin. I laid down and went to sleep, and when I woke up, he was inside me. I didn't know how to feel, like is this supposed to be how this happens. I felt afraid because I was a Christian, my family is Christian. I was so afraid to tell my family what happened. But years later, I had to tell them. From that I grew stronger and began to affirm myself. I prayed more and I knew I could bounce back!

B: How would you encourage a single mother that feels defeated?

D: Take care of yourself first! If something happens to you, who does that leave your kids too. There were times where I cried about my health, not having a man there to help me. I wished I had a seizure and died. But I made it through prayer.

I encourage you also because Moms feel judged at times, but you have to find someone to talk to. It doesn't have to be family but find a friend that will let you let it all out. My friend lets me vent and then they remind me that I am a good mother.

Prayer of Self-Acceptance

Lord, I praise You because I am fearfully and wonderfully made by You! Your works are marvelous, and my soul knows this full well! (Psalm 139:13-14) Before You formed me in my mother's womb You knew me. You perfectly created me in your very image.

Therefore, I accept the truth of Your word concerning my life, my family, my finances, my health, my heart, and my perception of myself. I reject every lie from the enemy, and I stand on the word of God, which is sharper than any two-edged sword. (Hebrews 4:12)

Father God, I accept how you created me. I will not lean to my own understanding, but I will acknowledge you in all that I do. (Proverbs 3:6) I fully embrace all that I am in You. I decree and declare that I am perfectly complete in You.

I walk in self-acceptance and in Your perfect love.

In Jesus' Name,
Amen.

Chapter 3:

It Just Got REAL!

I knew that life would change after marriage, which was easily accepted. However, after having two children back-to-back, I was not ready for the harsh reality that my emotions were changing for the worse. You hear about depression creeping in, but you never think it would happen to you.

Well, it did, known by the name of postpartum depression. Again, just like the c-section, no one in my family had been through this either. Or if they had, no one mentioned their experience. Here I am going through it, and I felt alone. I kept quiet for so long because I really didn't want to admit that I felt that way. I thought most people would think I was crazy. But had I opened up and spoken out about how I felt, I am sure, there would have been others that may have said, wow, I am going through that too and we could have helped in each other's recovery. At the time, I attempted to suppress it and my feelings and emotions backfired. At that time postpartum depression was not something that people really spoke about.

As I went through it, I was very irritable. I would have extreme mood swings (some call it highs and lows), and I was not focused. My confidence was shaken; actually, at that time it was lacking. I tried the common cliche *fake it til you make it*, which didn't work.

I noticed that I was angry for silly reasons, which I couldn't even tell you why to this day. I became very impatient. I recall a situation where all I wanted to do was leave but my husband took his time. When we got in the car, I unleashed a hurricane of emotions at him. I shouted, "Why couldn't you hurry up?! Couldn't you see I was ready to go?!" On and on I went. I was dead wrong and completely out of line. At the time I couldn't see it, and it didn't matter how he felt or what he was saying. I wanted to make him feel that his thoughts, feelings, or gestures did not matter.

There would be times where I needed to be in complete control that was totally unnecessary; I had other emotions as well. I was also afraid. Fear made me think I had no hope, like I should give up, but I knew I could never end my life. However, the majority of my emotions were based on anger, rejection, fear, and hopelessness, which led me to disconnect from those around me. I didn't want to be involved with people or my own work.

I knew then that it was time to seek help. The feeling of disconnection is never a good thing, especially when you have a family to care for. I never got to a place, thank God, where I wanted to harm my children, husband, or myself. However, there are some women who battle postpartum depression that do feel the need, or urge, to harm those around them.

One Wednesday night at church another mother from our church asked:

S: How are you doing?

Me: (I didn't say it out loud, but honestly, I was thinking I'm a wreck), but I told her I was ok.

S: How are you really? She looked at me, in my eyes and past the mask I put up and saw my heart.

Me: I replied, "Not good; my emotions are everywhere, and I don't know what to do."

S: I will be praying for you.

She hugged me and we departed.

I definitely appreciated that! A few weeks after that, another sister in the church asked me the same question. I was honest and I owned it. She told me that after her babies came back-to-back, she too fought depression. Not only that, but that someone came to stay with her to make sure she was eating and taking care of herself while her husband was at work. Someone helped her care for the baby because she knew she needed help.

She told me she would pray for me as well, but she also told me to journal. I thought, *Journal? Why?* Although uncertain as to why I needed to journal, I did it. I trusted the word of God that came from her, and this is how the book was birthed. I began to write and pray, and God began to open doors. He connected me with doctors and other mothers who knew mothers that endured and fought this battle as well.

Back to Wednesday night, mother number one came up to me and asked how I was, and I responded better than I was. She said ok, and that she would continue to pray for me. Little did we both know, there was a news report that very week, of a mother who had experienced postpartum psychosis. That mother had an episode, and it was blasted on the news stations. From that situation, I realized, God was speaking to me, to finish this book.

I have heard several reports of new mothers and women that have lost control of their emotions and have hurt themselves and hurt their families as well. There have been moments of feeling like I hate myself, or being rude and obnoxious to others, but at my weakest moment, there was always someone who did or said something to bring me back. Bring me back to a place of peace or put me in a place of happiness and restoration.

I realize that others may not have that feeling of being supported, but let me remind you, there is always somewhere or someone that you can turn to, that will remind you that you are indeed NOT crazy. Because you are not! There must be balance in your life. You must trust others to help you and in trusting others, you must trust yourself to go through it!

"Weeping may endure for a night, but joy comes in the morning". Psalms 30:5 Fear, anger, hurt, pride, loneliness, may endure for just a little while, but please believe, you will receive your joy back! But there is a little fighting that must take place. You have to own your personal fight and be willing to go through the process. You can't blame others for what you are going through. You cannot make them feel bad because you are not managing your emotions.

Looking back on my process I can wholeheartedly say that I experienced postpartum depression. I had multiple symptoms and denial kept me from wanting to get the help that I should have sought after. I had to fight for my life and to take it back.

Many may ask what Postpartum depression looks like. Postpartum depression generally triggers after childbirth. It is a range of emotions that can fluctuate from joy to sorrow, anxiety to extreme peace, fear to anger, being in control to losing every capacity to love anything and anyone in sight. All those things should be red flags to you that there may be support that you should seek from others, if not your family, close friends, and most importantly, your physician or find a therapist. Sometimes we don't recognize them for ourselves.

So, before we continue in this conversation, I pray for the family and friends that are around you. That their minds, eyes, and hearts are open to see changes in you that could be signs of postpartum depression or any type of depression. I rebuke the thought that you may feel attacked by them. I pray that your family supports you with love and support as you need it. And I pray that you truly receive the support and when asked, that you are open and honest, so that you receive the needed help.
In Jesus name, Amen.

After researching several websites and speaking with physicians; most agreed that some signs might look like:

Mood swings to include worthlessness or guilt.

They can also be:

- Anxiety
- Sadness (feel like crying a lot)
- Irritability (also looks like lack of patience)
- Poor eating habits
- Crying
- Decreased concentration
- Trouble Sleeping
- Overly worried about the baby or not concerned at all about them.

Most of these last a few days, but some can last longer than a week or two. Postpartum affects a very small number of mothers. Some reports suggest that within the first 10 days after giving birth postpartum symptoms begin to show. Postpartum depression as well as Depression knows no color or race. It just happens. Symptoms can grow to be longer lasting and may sometimes interfere with the care for yourself or your own child. *(Mayo Medical Clinic)*.

The actual postpartum depression symptoms include:

- Loss of appetite
- Insomnia
- Intense irritability and anger
- Overwhelming fatigue
- Loss of interest in sex
- Lack of joy in life

Before I realized these things were going on in my life, I never really understood that this was a real thing. After watching the news and seeing reports of mothers who had moments where they were extremely overwhelmed and had other symptoms, I began to realize that this could be my reality. As hard as it was to accept, I knew deep down that their feelings were the same as mine.

The thought of harming my children really scares me. However, I had seen it on the news multiple times, so I knew that it was a real thing. I mean, I know sometimes I would be exhausted and dramatic, but I would NEVER intentionally harm them.

Most ladies mentioned that the support from their families helped in their healing and recovery. The ones who sought medical expertise found that helped in their long-term recovery. The recommendation from the mothers in the study was to always be open about your feelings, even if others did not understand; to find someone who does. They mentioned that they knew they were not "crazy", it was solely emotional things that they were going through.

I spoke with an amazing doctor. Throughout our conversation he shared several nuggets that helped me to understand the weight of this conversation.

B: What are the signs that you look for before diagnosing postpartum depression and postpartum psychosis?

Dr. B: His thoughts were that there is a risk of problems with the mother's mood and sleeping problems. Also, he mentioned that if there was a previous history of depression within the patients' family, there would be a greater risk of the mother falling into the realm of postpartum depression.

B: What are the differences between the two and how do you diagnose them?

Dr. B: Psychosis- seeing, hearing, or having delusional thoughts. Outward behavior, being out of touch with reality. Psychosis can come without depression. It is hard to pick up without mood problems.

B: Can postpartum depression be seen in the last stages of pregnancy?

Dr. B: Could not answer definitively

B: What is the PHQ9 (Patient Health Questionnaire)? How does using this questionnaire help new mothers or mothers in general? Is that an accurate study?

Dr. B: PHQ9, used to track treatments. When tracking them generally try to connect with the primary care physician to assist in treatments. The highest which is 20, means the person is severe. It is generally recommended that the treatment prescribed is psychotherapy or antidepressants for one month.

B: Can fathers develop postpartum symptoms? Is there help for them?
Dr. B: Theory is that there are more women than men. However, stress can lead to psychiatric symptoms.

B: After the six-week checkup, do you suggest that maybe a 9 or 12 week follow up for mothers would help detect postpartum symptoms?
Dr. B: Could not answer definitively
B: What is the time frame of when a mother can be diagnosed and how long does it last?
Dr. B: Within 6 weeks. Like other depression symptoms, it can last years if not treated.

B: What are the support systems that you would suggest to mothers and fathers?

Dr. B: His first thoughts would be to refer them to the YMCA or Planned Parenthood.

I truly agree with him, especially with the last question. There are plenty of organizations which you can get involved in that would be of great support to you and your family. The Momm-E friends suggested that although all support is not good support, you must seek out and find what support works for you. We are all fearfully and wonderfully made (Psalm 139:14), but that does not mean what worked for me, will work for you. Nor does it mean what I went through or how I felt, will feel the same to you.

"You do NOT have to suffer in silence or feel ashamed. Our babies need us to be healthy during a time when we are overwhelmed the most".

-Brittany Willow Mayer

Conversation with a Mother of Young Children:

B: Did you experience depression after the birth of your children?

L: I did and do. I experienced extreme sadness. I felt like I wasn't good enough, like I did not know what I was doing.

B: How is having 3 children under 5 years old?

L: It can be busy. Three different needs. Three different emotions. Talk to me, play with me, hold me. It can be demanding.

B: How do you handle the demand?

L: I teach them not to shout. We all take a moment. You know, the baby needs more attention. So, I let them know their father is there also.

B: How old are your children?

L: 4 years old, 3 years old, and 8 months

B: Have you ever felt like giving up?

L: I've had moments where I shut down. Like, don't ask me for anything, don't even look at me. But then I step back and look at their faces and it melts my heart all over again.

I constantly remind myself that QUITTING is not an option. Pull it together, you have got to get this done.

B: Were their people to help you get through it?

L: There were women that I would talk to about it. Once, I talked about it, it wasn't as bad as I made it out to be. Here I am making the most out of things and my people would talk me off the edge.

Conversation of a Mother that has Battled Depression:

B: How do you manage being a mom to 3 kids of various ages?

M: I don't manage! I tackle my days, one at a time! And try to plan ahead. I also try to check in with them emotionally, mentally, and physically with each child and also check my emotions. So that I can be present for them.

I MUST get my emotions together.

B: Have you ever experienced postpartum depression or any type of depression?

M: Absolutely

B: How did you get through it?

For me it took acknowledging I don't have to be everything to everybody! It took counseling, therapy, and prayer.

B: How are you feeling now?

M: I still battle depression. I still go to therapy. I know my triggers. I am a spiritual person, so I always pray and listen to sermons, praise, and worship to keep me fighting.

B: What does balance look like to you? Being a wife, mother, and business owner.

M: It looks like unplugging. I do what I have to do for my mental state. I have to remember, no one is coming to save you, so you must save yourself. Save yourself Sis!

__Conversation with Mother of a High School Boy__

B: What is your greatest fear as a mother?

H: After I was thrust it into the single parent roll, (pre-pandemic) I just wanted the Lord to protect my children and allow them to come home every day. Come home from school, from church, and now that my oldest is working, from work. That was and still is my greatest fear as a black mother of 2 strong and intelligent black boys.

And a close second is that my children will say I never taught them anything as a mother.

B: How old are your children?

H: 13 and 16

B: How is it being a boy mom?

H: That's the question of the century. Being a mother to boys is unique. As a mother, I cannot raise them to be men. I don't think a woman can teach a boy to be a man, just my thoughts. I can teach them how to treat women and men, to be respectful, how to walk, talk, and carry themselves. I have men in my life to help teach them how to be men. Nothing is censored in my house. All the body sounds and all.

B: Do you feel like you attain your goals?

H: Career goals, yes, I met them. But I can always grow. I'll never stop learning in the medical field. I thought I was reaching my spiritual goal for that time period while continuing to set goals for the next. We must continue to learn on a spiritual level. But it was not until something very drastic happened in my life a few years ago when I lost.... my "spiritual gusto".

I was very mad at God. I started to question God. I'd ask over and over why such a thing could happen to me. I don't bother anybody. I stay busy taking care of my family and being a mom. A wife. A Christian. So, to answer your question I have not met my spirit goal.... yet!!!!

B: Do you feel the anger you had is gone?

H: I'm working on it.

Prayer of Peace

Father, in the name of Jesus, I declare that your peace rules in my heart and mind. Jehovah Shalom, take control of every chaotic situation in my life. Dispatch your warring angels to fight on my behalf against every demonic force that will attempt to rob me of the peace that you have ordained for me.

According to Philippians 4:7, I decree that the peace which surpasses all understanding is manifesting in my life. I renounce worrying, anxiousness, fear, doubt, chaos, confusion, calamity, and any other spirit that has come to rob me of my peace. I declare that you will keep me in perfect peace because my mind is stayed on you. (Isaiah 26:3) Thank you, Prince of Peace, for causing me to triumph in every situation.

In Jesus' Name,
Amen.

Prayer for Forgiveness

*Lord, forgive me for the things that I have done and said that have hurt my family and friends. Those actions were unbecoming of who you made me to be. Help them to forgive me as well.
And if they will not forgive me, help me to be ok and at peace with their decision.*

Help me to speak as you would have me to speak. For your word declares a soft answer turns away wrath! I thank you that wrath no longer lives in my heart, nor my mouth. The seeds of anger, hatred, and confusion have been removed from my heart.

Lord help to listen to You first, before speaking. Order my steps so that I may do what is pleasing unto you! And when I do what pleases you, I know that my actions toward family and friends will be right.

Thank you for the spirit of conviction that's within me.

In Jesus Name,

Amen

Chapter 4:

Walking in Victory

Every day I wake up to new mercies! Not to say that every day, in its entirety, was going to be peaches and cream, but I knew that in order for me to walk in victory, my mindset had to change. I could no longer allow my thoughts to control me. I could no longer allow the feelings of anger to control my life nor my day.

When you recognize the issues that you face, you then must take ownership, address them, and move forward. I know when you go through something as major as depression; you ask yourself what would I be like after? Well, you will be yourself, but better. Meaning growth has taken place. You will become more aware in recognizing your triggers, better in your response to situations, better all the way around. With the help of my family, friends, and most importantly, God, I was able to crush every issue that I faced. Now, there will be times where you fall back, but that is a part of growth as well.

Growth doesn't happen overnight. It is a slow and steady process. My family and close friends helped me grow daily by reminding me of who I was and who I could become. I know everyone does not have the family or friend's support that I do, but you need to get you some folks around you that will be honest with you.

I had to do specific things to propel my growth. I order for you to grow you have got to do something. You can't stay where you are because you will never change! My growth started as I increased my prayer life. If you pray, continue to seek God for healing, guidance, and strength. He will direct your actions. Something can be finding a workout class at a community center, something can be going back to school to take a class, and something can be picking up a trade that you never knew was within you. Do something to empower you to be better. Doing things does not always require money that is spent, trust me, I don't have much, but I will make time to do **SOMETHING** for myself!

Take walks in the park; hang out at the local coffee house. Attend a church function; connect with the mothers at the library where you bring your child for story time; go to the dog park. There are always things to do.

Our walks will show a different form of victory, but as long as you walk tall, you will be victorious! Doctors are always there for support. My opinion is that if you consult with your doctor with full transparency, which means, being open and honest, they will lead you in the right direction. I say full transparency because I told my doctors that I was ok, or good sometimes, knowing that was definitely not the case. In other words, I lied to myself and them, to make it seem as if things were ok. I was crying and literally dying on the inside. I was honestly lying to myself, knowing I needed desperately to connect with someone. Honesty is always best. If you cannot be honest with family or friends you will never walk in victory, because your lies will compound, and it will be hard for you to be free.

I recall one Sunday morning service. I was really battling with my feelings and emotions. Our Bishop said "Life and freedom are what God gives you, however, you must first fully submit to Him. But if you don't submit, you have made the choice to stay in what you are in." That hit me like a ton of bricks! I mean I was so weighted down, that I was not paying attention to the fact that I did not truly submit to God. At that moment, I submitted. And choose FREEDOM! After that, the weights, and pressures I felt had left.

And as you choose freedom, victory will soon follow. As I have dealt with and now been delivered from this post-partum issue, I have learned a few things about myself. I share with you, because you too, WILL overcome this!

I learned that Jesus loves me beyond anything I can think or believe about myself.

I learned to be more gracious and kinder towards my husband and family.

I learned to love more!

I learned that it is okay to be overwhelmed, but it is how you respond to the situation that will determine my outcome.

I learned that I am an amazing mother despite what the devil tried to put in my mind.

I learned that I have the POWER to speak life!

I learned that God has NOT given me the spirit of fear.

I learned that just because I share my feelings more does not mean that I am weak because I am stronger than I have ever been.

I learned that to be the best example, sometimes it is best to be quiet!

I learned to say thank you for the little things.

I learned to always be radical in my faith!

I learned that my stretch marks (yes honey, all of them) and weight change do not define how I should feel about myself.

I have learned these things, now I speak these things into you!
You are beautiful!
You will be the mother that is wise!
You will be the mother that educates her children!
Your children will rise and call you blessed!
Your past hurts combined with your thoughts of failure will propel you into greatness!
You have a sound mind!
You will be able to think and make wise decisions pertaining to life and not make hasty irrational decisions.
You will not be ashamed to share your past failures with others, because they can learn from you.
You are victorious!
You will not allow the images in social media to define what you should look like!

You will be free from generational curses that attempt to stifle your growth and your future!
You are a living testimony!
You will not be afraid to say that you are not ok!
You will receive the love of God!

There were a lot of things throughout this journey and one thing that sticks out most is to keep walking! That does not mean I am always physically walking; it means I am going forward toward my purpose. My thoughts about my purpose helps me to cultivate my children's purposes. Regardless of who I was in the past, I have walked right out of my past and into my future. A future of promise, radical faith, and unspeakable joy! Which are all things my children will feel and see.

While walking I've noticed there is a sense of freedom that I have. I say freedom because in the past I was bound by the thoughts of my mind and what I felt in my heart. My mind had huge control of me, and I allowed that one thought (seed) to grow. And that one seed grew so much that I could not control the various thoughts I had. The devil had me so bound and he made me think it was ok to live and treat people the way I did. I hated the person I was then!

And today, I am MUCH different. I am happy, loved and make all attempts to share the love with others that God gives me daily, and I thank God every day that I was able to choose to live in FREEDOM! I walk daily in victory and freedom!

I thank God that I am free!

This feels so good to me.

"Victory is reserved for those who are willing to pay its price."

-Sun Tzu

Prayer of Freedom

"If the Son therefore shall make you free, ye shall be free indeed." ~John 8:36

Father, forgive me of every sin that I have committed. Purge me with hyssop, give me a clean heart, and renew a right spirit within me.

I renounce all demonic bondages, spirits of rebellion and disobedience, illegal soul ties, and all forms of idolatry. I declare that you are the Lord of my life and the lover of my soul. I walk in your forgiveness and freedom, in Jesus' Name.

I will resist the devil and he shall flee from me! I lay aside every weight and the sin that easily besets me. I walk in continual spiritual freedom and deliverance. Thank you, Lord, for restoration, revival, salvation, correction, refocusing, and refilling of your Holy Spirit.

In Jesus' Name,
Amen.

Prayer of Thanksgiving

"In everything give thanks: for this is the will of God in Christ Jesus concerning you."
~I Thessalonians 5:18

Father, I thank You! Thank You for Your unfailing love. Thank You for Your unending grace and mercy. Thank You for Your presence, guidance, and protection.

Thank You for provision and prosperity. Thank You for the manifestation of Your promises. Thank You for abundant life. Thank You for favor, for it is better than life. Thank You for Your faithfulness.

Thank you for the harvest. Thank you for giving us power through Your name, and for allowing us to exercise that power through prayer. Thank you, Lord!

In Jesus' Name,
Amen.

Words of Encouragement and Gratitude:

Many of you are not aware, but we suffered the loss of a baby last April. It was a difficult moment, yet one filled with hope and promise. God showed us that He was in control, in the face of the doctor's diagnosis and science.

Prior to this, I was diagnosed with polycystic ovarian syndrome (PCOS). The doctors informed us that we would have difficulty conceiving, and even if we did conceive, we would not be able to carry to full term.

However, I am so glad that we serve GOD who does not deal in uncertainty and what-ifs. He is the God of our YES! He is a God who can do all things but fail! We returned to the doctor last October and for the first time we heard the words, everything looked great. God healed my body!

All things happened in God's timing. After that visit in October, within a month's time, our little nugget was conceived. We confirmed the good news on Christmas Eve.

For the trial and the testimony, we say Thank You Lord!

To some this may be TMI or over sharing, but we are overcome by the blood of the lamb and the words of our testimonies. All that we endure is to the glory of God! Many of us hold keys to another's deliverance or ability to find faith again, but we sit on the testimony. In sharing, we hope that our story can encourage someone else in some way.

God is not a man that He should lie, nor a son of man that He should repent; Has he said, and He not do it? Or has he spoken, and He will not make it good? Numbers 23:19

Whatever your promise is, the word you've been holding on to is He said, He will make it Good! God is about to make good on His word.

The Freemans

Closing Prayer:

Lord, we thank You for the words of expression. We thank you for freeing us from anger, pride, confusion, shameful thinking, and not walking fully in Your promise. We recognize where we were and the steps, we have taken to become who we are now. Today we are ALL victorious!

Our minds are clear and no longer filled with the thoughts of confusion that have triggered negative responses in our lives. For we walk in truth, we walk in happiness, and we walk stronger so that our children can be free.

"I'm free indeed, through Christ I'm free indeed. No chains are holding me, that's who I choose to be". I'm free, praise the Lord I'm free, no longer bound, no more chains holding me!

We thank You for Your word that reminds us, whom the son set free, is free indeed!

Your love is never-ending. Teach us how to love unconditionally, as you love us.

Thank you for each reader. May their understanding be expanded through the various conversations and their hearts grow more compassionate for those who have endured in silence.

Let the words of our mouths, and the meditation of our hearts, be acceptable in Your sight. Oh Lord, our Strength, and our Redeemer.

In Jesus, mighty Name we pray.
Amen

Made in the USA
Columbia, SC
29 June 2023